Light

Graham Peacock

Wayland

Titles in the series:

ASTRONOMY • ELECTRICITY • FORCES
GEOLOGY • HEAT • LIGHT • MATERIALS
METEOROLOGY • SOUND • WATER

Editor: Kate Asser
Series Designer: Jan Sterling, Sterling Associates
Book Designer: Joyce Chester

This edition published in 1995 by
Wayland (Publishers) Ltd

First published in 1993 by
Wayland (Publishers) Ltd
61 Western Road, Hove
East Sussex, BN3 1JD, England

British Library Cataloguing in Publication Data
Peacock, Graham
Light. – (Science Activities Series)
I. Title   II. Series
535

HARDBACK ISBN 0-7502-0697-7

PAPERBACK ISBN 0-7502-1689-1

Acknowledgements
The publishers would like to thank the following for allowing their
pictures to be used in this book: Eye Ubiquitous *Cover (right)* (Paul
Seheult); Natural History Photographic Agency *Cover (top)*; Science Photo
Library p22 (David Parker); Tony Stone Worldwide p5; Zefa p29.
All commissioned photographs are from the Wayland Picture Library
(Zul Mukhida). All artwork is by Tony de Saulles.

The publishers would also like to thank Stacey Eastap and Miles Fisher,
and their families, for their co-operation and help in making this book.

Typeset by Dorchester Typesetting Group Ltd
Printed and bound in Italy by G. Canale & C.S.p.A.

Contents

Words that appear in **bold** are explained in the glossary
on page 30.

Travelling light

It is light that allows us to see. Most light comes to us from the sun. When it hits something, it is bounced back again in different directions, and some of it enters our eyes. Our eyes send messages to our brain, which makes pictures from the light, so that we know what is in front of us. When it is dark, there is no light to be bounced back into our eyes, so we do not see anything.

Which things can light pass through?

You will need:

different kinds of paper

1 Hold up a piece of paper to the light. Can you see light through it?

2 How many times can you fold the paper and still see light through it?

3 Which kinds of paper are easy to see through? Which kinds of paper are impossible to see through?

Transparent things let most light pass through them. Plain glass and clear plastic are both transparent.

Translucent things let some through. Most paper is translucent.

Opaque things do not let any light through. Wood and thick card are both opaque.

Sweet dreams

Do an experiment to find out which fabric would make the best curtains.

Why are some shadows darker than others?

Use a torch to make **shadows** in different places around a room. Where are the shadows darkest and sharpest? Where are they fuzzy and light?

Make sharp shadows
Shine a torch at a small object in a box. Notice that the torch, the object and the shadow are all in line with each other.

◄ *During an eclipse, the moon blocks out light from the sun.*

Straight Light travels in straight lines. When an object gets in the way, a shadow is formed. When light comes from several places the shadows are fuzzy and indistinct.

Fast Light travels faster than anything else in the universe. It takes only one second to travel 300,000 km.

300,000 km

Seeing clearly

You will need:

◆ **a mirror** ◆ **a pencil** ◆ **some paper**

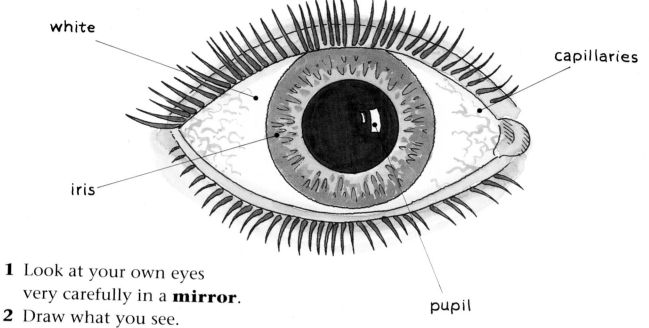

white

capillaries

iris

pupil

1 Look at your own eyes
   very carefully in a **mirror**.
2 Draw what you see.

Pupils

Flash a torch into someone's eye. What
do you notice happens to the **pupil**?
The pupil controls the amount of light
that enters the eye. In bright light the
pupil does not need to be as large as it
does in dim light.

Blinking

Every time you blink, your **eyelids**
clean your eyes. If you did not blink,
dust and dirt would stay in your eyes
and might damage them.

Time how long you can go without
blinking.

Did you know?

Fish don't have eyelids.

Birds have two sets of
eyelids. One goes across
the eye and the other goes
up and down.

How well can you see?

1 Stand about two metres away from this book.

2 Close one eye. How far down the chart can you read?

3 Try the other eye. Is that eye better or worse?

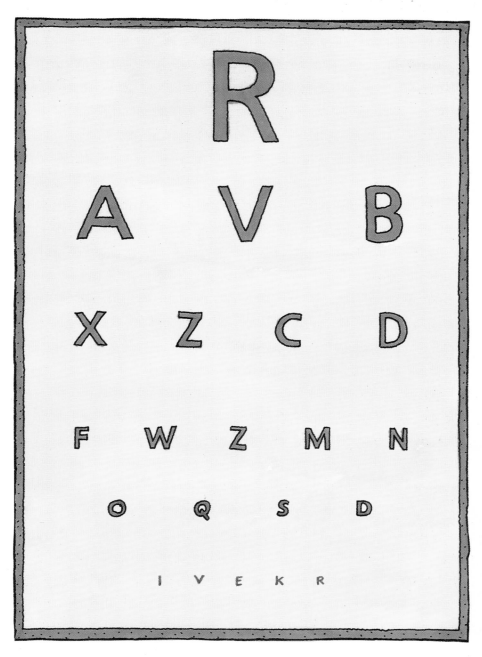

Not everyone's eyes are the same. Sometimes eyes that belong to the same person are different from each other.

How close can you get?

1 How close to this page can you get before the writing goes fuzzy?

2 Test each eye. Which one can get the closest before the writing goes fuzzy?

Don't believe your eyes

Which red line in each pair is the longest?

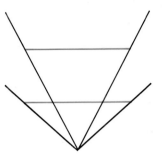

Check with a ruler.

Are the red lines parallel? ▼

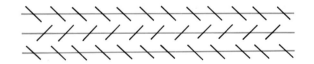

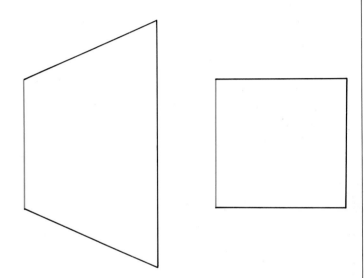

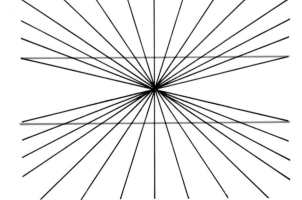

Use your ruler to check.

Blind spot

1   Cover your right eye.

2   Stare at the cross with your left eye.

3   Slowly move towards the page.

4   The spot should disappear when you are about 20 cm from the page.

How do cartoons work?

You will need:

* scissors * paper * a pencil
* sticky tape or stapler

1 Cut out two pieces of paper about 6 cm square.

2 Draw a bird on one piece and a cage on the other.

3 Staple or stick the sides and top together and fix them on to the end of a pencil.

4 Spin the pencil between your hands and watch what happens to the bird.

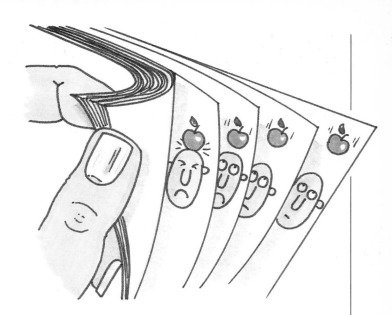

You will need:

* a pencil * a notebook

1 Draw a series of pictures, all slightly different, in the corner of the notebook.

2 Flick the corner of the book and watch the **cartoon** move.

Cinema films are made from a series of still pictures. Things seem to move because the next picture appears just as the last one fades. The pictures change too fast for the eye to notice that they are separate.

Using two eyes

Why do we need two eyes?

1 Close one eye.

2 Watch a friend move their finger near your face.

3 When their hand is still, try to touch their fingertip with yours.

You need two eyes to judge the distance and position of things, because each eye gives you a different view of an object.

1 Close one eye.

2 Hold your finger at arm's length and look at it with the open eye.

3 Change eyes. What do you notice?

How far round can you see?

1 Sit in a chair.

2 Keep your head still.

3 How far can you see to each side?

4 Draw a plan showing what you can see.

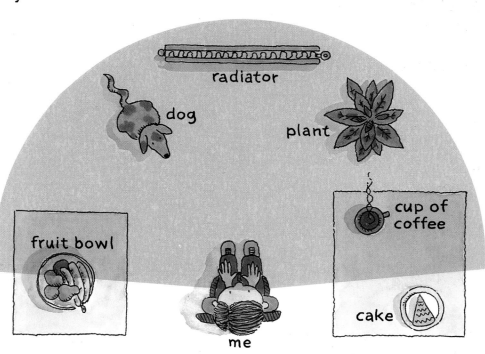

Hunters and hunted

Animals that hunt have eyes which point forward to give them the best view of their prey.

Animals that are hunted have eyes on the sides of their head, so that they can see danger coming from all directions.

Which of these animals are hunters?

Flat mirrors

How do mirrors work?

You will need:
- a small mirror
- an elastic band
- a small box
- a torch
- a comb made from a cereal box

1 Hold the mirror upright by attaching it to the box with the elastic band.
2 Darken the room.
3 Shine the torch at the mirror through the comb.
4 Move the torch and comb. Watch what happens to the path of the light the mirror shines back.

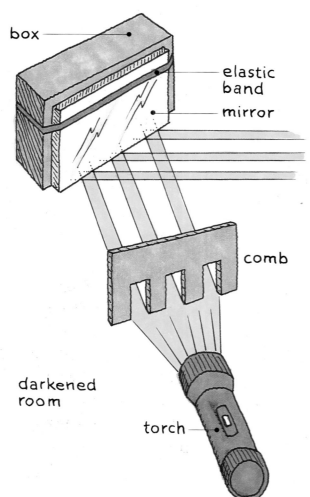

box

elastic band

mirror

comb

darkened room

torch

Left to right

1 Look into a mirror.
2 Wave at yourself with your left hand.
3 Notice that in the mirror, you are waving back with your right hand. The mirror has turned you round.

Rough and smooth

Rough surfaces scatter light in all directions.

Mirrors and other very smooth surfaces **reflect** light in one direction.

More illusions

The candle seems to be burning inside the glass of water.

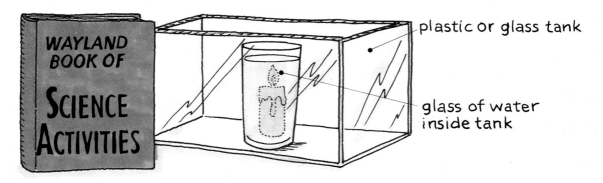

plastic or glass tank

glass of water inside tank

Set up the trick like this:

You will need:

- a candle
- a glass of water
- a glass tank
- a book to act as a screen

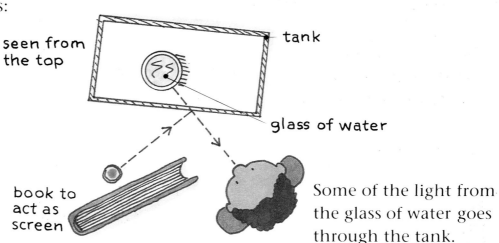

seen from the top

tank

glass of water

Some of the light from the candle is reflected off the tank.

book to act as screen

Some of the light from the glass of water goes through the tank.

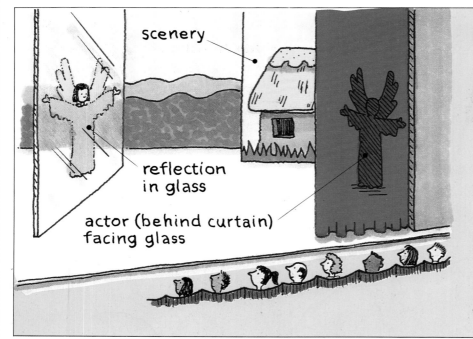

scenery

reflection in glass

actor (behind curtain) facing glass

Did you know?

This trick was invented by an actor about 100 years ago. He hung a sheet of glass on stage and stood in the wings under bright lighting, dressed as a ghost. To the audience it looked as if there was a ghost on stage. The trick is known as Pepper's ghost.

Two mirrors

You will need:

- two mirrors ◆ sticky tape
- a small toy

1   Hinge the mirrors together with the sticky tape.

2   Stand the toy in the angle between the mirrors.

3   Count the **reflections** you can see.

4   What happens to the number of reflections if you move the mirrors closer together or further apart?

Now stand the mirrors opposite each other.

How many reflections can you see this time?

Did you know?

The first mirrors were made of polished metal. Modern mirrors are made of a very thin layer of silver coated on to glass. They were invented in Germany in 1835.

The reflection in a mirror is called the **image**.

In these activities the image is reflected backwards and forwards between the two mirrors.

How do kaleidoscopes and periscopes work?

Kaleidoscope

You will need:

- two long, thin mirrors
- some card
- greaseproof paper or tissue paper
- sticky tape
- beads or scraps of coloured paper
- a light

1 Tape the mirrors together down their long side.

2 Join the open sides with a piece of card.

3 Fix the greaseproof paper or tissue paper over one end with the sticky tape.

4 Put the beads or scraps of paper in the kaleidoscope. Hold it over the light and look at the patterns.

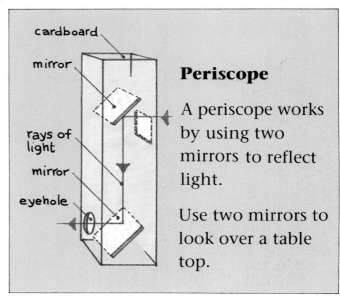

cardboard

mirror

rays of light

mirror

eyehole

Periscope

A periscope works by using two mirrors to reflect light.

Use two mirrors to look over a table top.

Curved mirrors

What can you see in convex mirrors?

Mirrors that curve outwards are called convex mirrors. They give a very wide view and are used for mirrors in cars and shops.

1 Look for shiny things that curve outwards.

2 Draw what you see in some of them.

In convex mirrors the image is always the right way up.

The screen of a television that is switched off works like a big curved mirror.

Did you know?

The English word 'pupil' comes from the French word for doll, because your reflection in someone's pupil looks like a doll.

What can you see in concave mirrors?

Mirrors that curve inwards are called concave mirrors. They make a close up object look bigger. The image from an object at a distance is small and upside-down.

Headlamps and torches

Torches and car headlamps use concave mirrors for their reflectors. Concave mirrors produce a strong beam of light which goes in one direction.

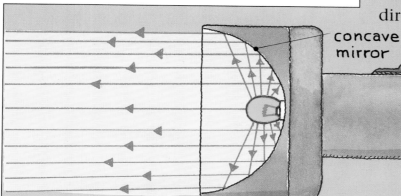

concave mirror

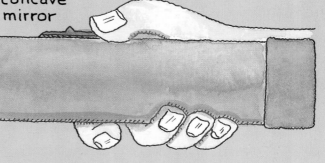

The biggest

Huge concave mirrors are used in telescopes. They gather and **focus** the light. The biggest concave telescope mirror is in the USA. It is over 10m in diameter and is made up from 36 smaller mirrors.

Focusing heat

Light and heat from the sun can be focused by curved mirrors to heat up water to make electricity.

1 Hold a shiny spoon at arm's length, with the bowl facing you.

2 Slowly bring the bowl of the spoon right up to your eye. What do you notice happens to the image as it comes closer to you?

Bending light

Magnify your finger

Put your finger into a glass of water. Can you see that your finger is **magnified** by the water?

What do you think causes this?

Appearing coin

You will need:

◆ a coin ◆ a shallow dish ◆ some water

1 Put the coin at the bottom of the dish.
2 Stand back, so the coin is just hidden by the rim of the dish.
3 Stay in the same place while a friend pours some water carefully into the dish. The coin reappears.

Do you get the same effect with an empty glass?

Do you notice a similar effect in a flat-sided tank of water?

Do magnifying lenses have to be made from glass?

You will need:
- ◆ **some cling film**
- ◆ **an old newspaper**
- ◆ **some water**

1 Put a piece of cling film over the newspaper.

2 Pour some water on to the cling film.

3 What happens to the writing underneath the water?

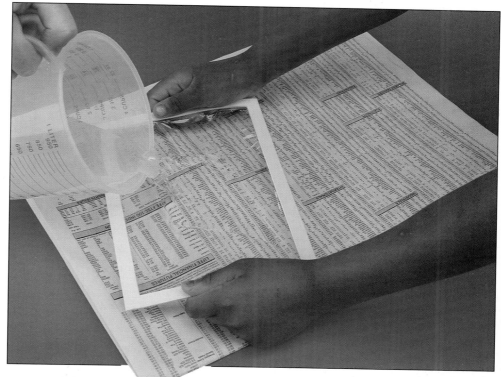

A piece of broken glass left in the countryside will act as a magnifying glass. It will focus light from the sun on to an object beneath it. If the sun is hot enough, the object may catch fire.

Slowing down light

When light goes from air into water or glass, it slows down. This makes it bend. When the light comes out of the glass into air, it speeds up again. This time it is bent the other way. This is called refraction.

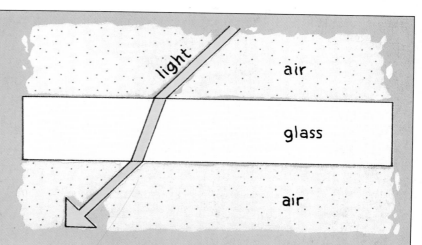

Cameras

Make a pinhole camera

You will need:

* a clean, safe tin * grease-proof paper * a source of light * an elastic band

1 Ask an adult to make a small hole in the bottom of the tin, with a hammer and a nail.

2 Fit the greaseproof paper over the open end of the tin, to make a screen. Hold it in place with an elastic band.

3 Point the small hole at a lamp, a bright window or a lighted candle. What do you see on the greaseproof paper screen? You may have to shield the screen by using a tube of news-paper or black paper.

Light travels in straight lines

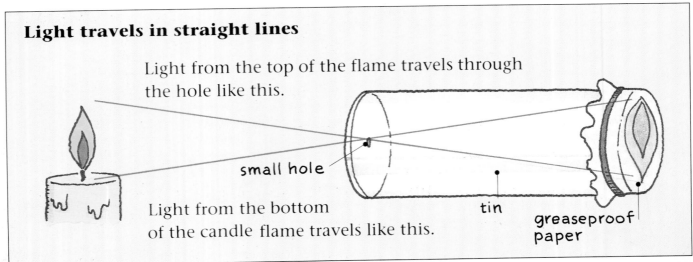

Light from the top of the flame travels through the hole like this.

small hole

Light from the bottom of the candle flame travels like this.

tin

greaseproof paper

How does a camera lens focus light?

1 Hold a lens at arm's length. What can you see?

2 Bring it closer. What happens now?

Make an image with a lens

You will need:

- some paper
- a lens
- a bright window

1 Hold the piece of paper facing the window.

2 Hold the lens between the paper and the window.

3 Carefully move the lens backwards and forwards until you can see a sharp image of the window on the paper.

A camera lens focuses light on to a film. The image on the film is upside-down like the image on the paper.

Did you know?

Fat lenses magnify things more strongly than thin lenses.

Fat lenses bend light more than thin lenses.

Rainbows and filters

How can you make a rainbow?

1 Put a dish of water in strong sunlight. Hold a mirror in the water so that it reflects the light. Gently tilt the mirror until bands of coloured light appear on the ceiling or wall.

2 Hold a **prism** in sunlight. Direct the light coming from it on to a wall or piece of paper.

3 Place a prism on the glass of an overhead projector. Move it until you can see a spectrum.

A prism will split white light into a rainbow.▶

Rainbows

Rainbows are formed when sunlight shines through droplets of water in the air. The sun is always behind you when you can see a rainbow.

White light

Light looks white to the human eye. However, light is really made up of different colours. When light goes through a prism the white light is split into the colours of the **spectrum**. Each colour of light is slowed down and bent by the plastic or glass. The red light is bent least, whilst the violet light is bent most.

What happens when you look through coloured filters?

1 Hold up a **filter** made from a piece of green see-through plastic against a white background.

What colour of light reaches your eye?

What do you think happens to all the other colours of light?

2 Try the same thing with a red filter.

3 Now hold up both the filters so that they overlap.
Why do you think that the area where they overlap appears black?

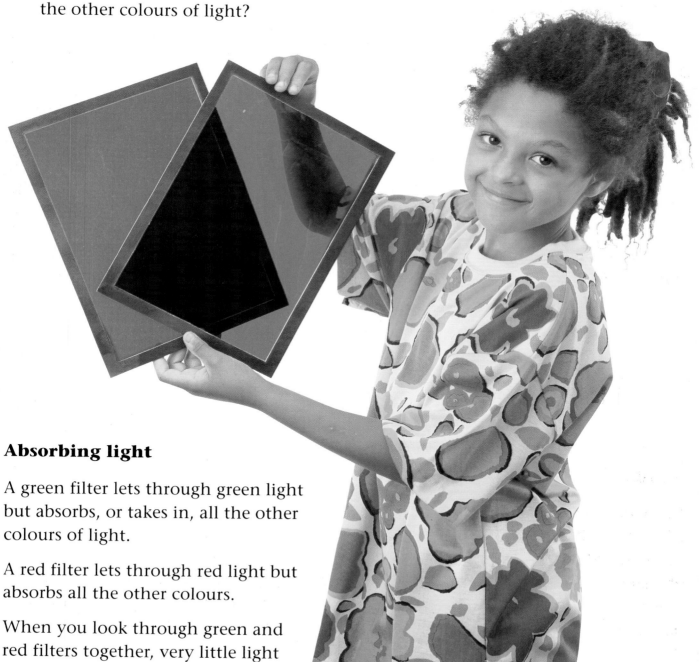

Absorbing light

A green filter lets through green light but absorbs, or takes in, all the other colours of light.

A red filter lets through red light but absorbs all the other colours.

When you look through green and red filters together, very little light gets through to your eye.

Coloured light

You will need:
- 3 torches
- blue, green and red filters
- different-coloured objects

1 Cover each torch with a different-coloured filter.

2 Work in a very dark room, or under a table shaded with black paper or black cloth.

3 Shine the coloured light from one of your torches on to the coloured objects.

4 Record what you notice.

Street lamps

Under yellow street lamps, red and blue cars look almost black.

Coloured shadows

Make coloured shadows like this:

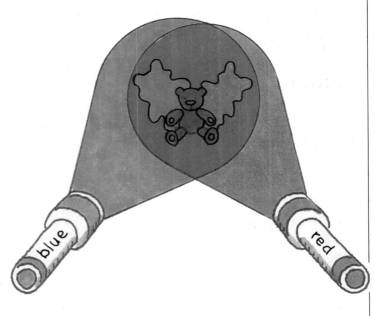

Can you explain what you see?

What colours do you get when you mix coloured light?

You will need:

● 3 torches ● blue, green and red filters ● white paper

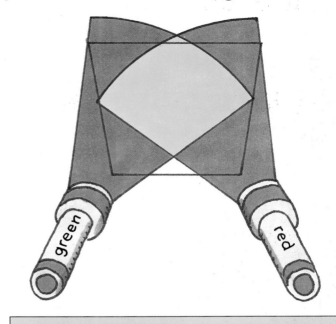

1 Cover each torch with a different filter.

2 In a very dark room, shine a green light and a red light on to the same piece of white paper. What happens to the colour of the paper?

3 Do the same with red and blue lights, and then with blue and green lights.

4 What colour do you get when you mix red, green and blue lights together?

To help the light mix, put thin white plastic under the filter. It helps to scatter the light.

Primary colours

Red, green and blue are the **primary colours** of light. You can make all the other colours by mixing the primary colours together in the right amounts. The primary colours themselves cannot be made from the other colours.

Spinner mix

Cut out circles of card about 10cm across. Colour them in sections, using felt-tip pens or crayons. Push an old pencil through the middle.

Spin each card. What colours can you make?

Television lights

How do colour televisions work?

1 Use a magnifying glass to look very closely at a colour television screen when it is switched on. Can you see that the picture is made up from tiny dots of coloured light?

2 What combination of dots makes up white parts of the picture? What combination of dots do you need to make up the other colours?

True or false?

1 Light travels faster than anything else.
2 You can see through opaque things.
3 Fish have two sets of eyelids.
4 You can judge distance as easily with one eye closed.
5 A kaleidoscope is used to see over the top of tall objects.
6 Owls are hunters. They have two forward-facing eyes.
7 A red filter absorbs blue light.
8 A concave mirror can focus light.
9 The image in a pinhole camera is the right way up.

All the answers are in this book.

Why do wheels sometimes seem to go backwards on television?

1 Wave your hand in front of the picture on a television screen. What do you notice?

2 Cut a propeller shape and fix it on to a piece of wood with a drawing pin.

3 Hold the propeller in front of the screen and spin it. What effects can you get by spinning it at different speeds?

Attach a soft weight, such as a small roll of sticky tape, to a piece of string about 20 cm long. Twirl the string in front of a bright screen, as below. What effect can you see?

Did you know?

The picture on a television screen is made up from 25 still pictures every second, but our eyes cannot detect this. To them, it seems that the same picture is moving.

Visibility and warning

Which colours would you use for a road sign?

You will need:

⬥ scissors ⬥ different-coloured paper ⬥ glue ⬥ a pencil

1 Cut out shapes from different-coloured paper. Make them all the same size.

2 Stick the shapes on to other pieces of coloured paper. Which colours show up the best?

3 Think of a test to see which colours would work best on a sign. Make sure the test is fair. Record your results on a graph.

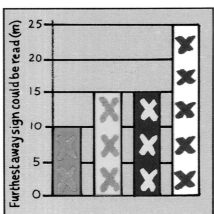

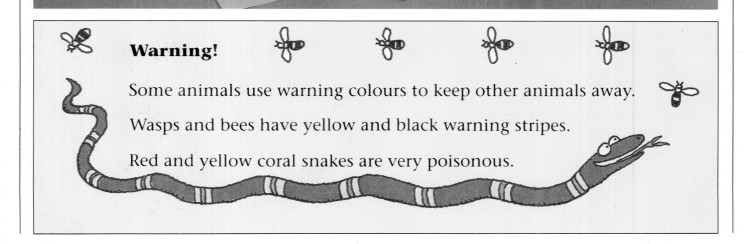

Warning!

Some animals use warning colours to keep other animals away.

Wasps and bees have yellow and black warning stripes.

Red and yellow coral snakes are very poisonous.

Which materials reflect light best at night?

1 Work in a dark room or make a dark box like this:

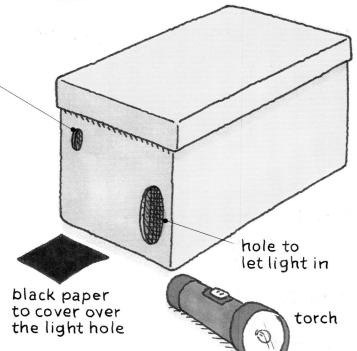

peephole

hole to let light in

black paper to cover over the light hole

torch

2 Put a few reflective objects in the box.
3 Look through the peephole. Cover over the light hole. Does anything show up in total darkness?

Which materials can you see in very dim light?

Which things show up best in the beam of a torch?

Collect reflective road safety materials and stickers. Which reflect light best?

Fluorescent and reflective
At night some materials, such as the stripes on a fireman's jacket, reflect light very well. **Fluorescent** materials absorb **ultra-violet light** and reflect well in dull light.

Firefighters wear reflective clothing so that they can be seen easily. ▼

Glossary

Blind spot   The part of the eye that has no nerve endings.

Capillaries   Small blood vessels.

Cartoon   A series of still pictures which are shown very quickly so that they look like a single moving picture.

Eyelids   The folds of skin that cover and protect the eye.

Filter   Something that allows only certain kinds of light to pass through.

Fluorescent   Fluorescent materials absorb part of light which we cannot normally see, called ultra-violet light, and change it into light we can see. This causes fluorescent materials to appear very bright.

Focus   To make light rays meet at a point.

Image   The reflection of an object in a mirror, or the view of it through a lens.

Iris   The coloured part of our eye. It is the muscle that closes or opens the pupil.

Magnified   To be made to look bigger.

Mirrors   Shiny flat surfaces that reflect images. Most mirrors are made of glass with a covering of silver on the back.

Opaque   Something that does not allow light to pass through.

Periscope   Something that uses two mirrors to reflect an image, so that you can see over things. They are used in submarines.

Primary colours   Colours that cannot be made by mixing other colours together. The primary colours of light are green, blue and red. These make secondary colours by adding other colours of light. The primary colours of paint are yellow, blue and red.

Prism   A triangular-shaped piece of glass or plastic.

Pupil   The hole in the centre of an eye which light passes through.

Rainbows   Bands of coloured light caused when sunlight shines through raindrops.

Reflect   To shine back from a surface.

Reflections   Images of an object that appear in mirrors, or on any shiny surfaces. Images are caused by the light rays from the object hitting the mirror, then bouncing back off it into your eye.

Shadows   Areas where there is little or no light.

Spectrum   The colours produced when white light is split up. The order of the colours is red, orange, yellow, green, blue, indigo, violet.

Translucent   Allowing only some light to pass through, so that things look fuzzy.

Transparent   Allowing all light to pass through, so that everything is clear.

Ultra-violet light   Rays of light, at the violet end of the spectrum, that we cannot normally see.

Books to read

Pocket Book of Science by Robin Kerrod (Kingfisher, 1990)
Jump! Science Books: Experiment with Light by Brian Murphy (Two Can, 1991)
Collins Primary Science by Linda Howe (Harper Collins, 1992)
100 Simple Science Experiments by Barbara Taylor (Kingfisher, 1990)
Science Starters: Colour and Light by Barbara Taylor (Franklin Watts, 1989)
Into Science: Light and Dark by Terry Jennings (Oxford, 1990)
My Science Book of Light by Neil Ardley (Dorling Kindersley, 1991)
Light and Seeing by David Crystal and John Foster (Hodder and Stoughton, 1991)

Notes for parents and teachers

Pages 4-5 When light passes through a material, some of it is absorbed and converted to heat energy. Different materials absorb different amounts of light. Opaque materials absorb the most light energy, and produce the most heat.

It is important for children to realize that shadows are not concrete, but an absence of light. The fact that the shadow is in line with the object and the torch shows that light travels in straight lines.

Light normally travels in straight lines, but it can be bent when it passes near very powerful sources of gravity.

Pages 6-7 Older people lose the ability to focus on very close objects, so the difference in sight between children and adults is likely to be significant.

Pages 8-9 The blind spot in our eyes is the place on the light-sensitive retina where the optic nerve leads to the brain. It is not sensitive to light, therefore light that falls there does not form an image and cannot send messages to the brain.

Page 10-11 Eyes that point forward provide stereoscopic sight, which is useful for judging distances. Humans probably developed stereoscopic sight in the early stages of their evolution, while they lived in trees.

Pages 12-13 Light is always reflected at the same angle at which it hits the reflecting surface, but in the opposite direction. Rays striking the surface from the far left will be reflected on the far right, which is why the image formed is reversed.

The Pepper's ghost effect is created because the bright light reflected on stage makes it difficult to see through the glass.

Pages 14-15 A crude periscope can be made with one mirror, but if two are used, the image produced is turned the right way round again.

Pages 16-17 It is important that children realize that parallel rays of light from a distant source are made to meet at the point of focus by a concave mirror. On the other hand, if a light source is placed at the point of focus, the rays reflected off the mirror are parallel.

Pages 18-19 The glass full of water gives the most distortion because the water affects the light more than the glass alone.

Light always bends when it enters a substance of a different density. If the substance is more dense, like the glass or water

here, its closely-packed molecules resist the light and slow it down, or bend it. This is called refraction. When the light passes back into the air, which is less dense, there is less resistance and it can speed up again, resuming its course.

Pages 20-21 The pinhole camera works best when you are looking at a brightly lit object. (You may also want to shade the screen.) The diagram at the bottom of the page explains why the image is inverted. If you make several holes in the camera, you will get several images.

Pages 22-23 The spectrum is formed because each band of coloured light travels at a different speed, or frequency, from the others. Red light is the slowest and violet the fastest. The difference is too minute to be seen unless the light is slowed down by refraction.

When light of different colours is absorbed by colour filters, the light energy is converted into heat energy. Pure filters are expensive, so if you use cheaper ones, it is a good idea to use them double, as this gives better results.

Pages 24-25 To make white light with the coloured torches you will need torches of equal brightness.

A spinner that gives pure white is hard to make, as the pigments in pens are impure.

The effect of colour is produced because a material reflects light of that frequency, or the primary colours that mix to form it, and absorbs the rest. A blue car under a yellow street light will look almost black because yellow light is made up of red and green light, which the blue car does not reflect well.

Pages 26-27 The image on a television screen is produced when the coloured dots on the screen are made to glow. A gun fires particles of electricity at the dots, crossing the screen 625 times for each separate image. Only dots that are struck by electrons glow, producing a different picture each time.

Pages 28-29 Visible light is only part of the full spectrum. There are other frequencies which the human eye cannot see. Ultra-violet light travels faster than violet light. Fluorescent materials absorb ultra-violet rays, and convert some of their energy to heat. When this happens, the rays are slowed down to a frequency that the human eye can see. This is the light which is reflected back, to give fluorescent materials their very bright colours.

Index